TABLE OF CONTENTS

Chapter 1 - You can be abundant with Real Estate

Chapter 2 - Why Buy Real Estate?

Chapter 3 - You don't need to be rich to build wealth with Real Estate

Chapter 4 - 5 Simple Steps to Financial Freedom

Chapter 5 - How to Buy Real Estate in Your Neighborhood with 30% or More Discount and Without Using Bank Credits

Chapter 6 - The Real Estate Business Is Done By Buying, Not By Selling

Chapter 7 - How to buy Real Estate so that you win even if the market goes down

Chapter 8 - Alternatives to bank financing

Chapter 9 - How to grow with Real Estate?

Chapter 10 - Final Conclusions

Many people think that doing something like this cannot be possible, due to the bad programming of their mind, and more specifically to the subconscious financial pattern that has been installed over the years in their brain, and that makes them think that buying Real Estate and multiplying wealth with them is not possible. So they make up all kinds of excuses for doing nothing, and they let opportunities slip right under their noses.

In fact, when an opportunity of this type presents itself, the voice of our unconscious always assails us with phrases such as:

- Now is not a good time

- You cannot do this, you are not prepared

- You don't have enough money

- It's not your time

- The market is dangerous

- You will lose everything

- You are not a smart investor

- You will make a serious mistake

However, the reality is that you can grow with Real Estate. And I will show you with this reason: how many of the most important things you have done, did you do without money, without contacts and without knowledge?

What I mean is that when you feel like it, you do what you want, regardless of your situation and the context that surrounds you.

There are people who raise their children no matter how, without having enough money, support or time. The circumstances were perhaps not favorable either, in fact they were just the opposite.

In the end we do things regardless of the resources we have, even without having great self-esteem at the time, but one decision changed everything. Perhaps it was also your case, do you remember that day when you made that decision that transformed your life?

So, if you want, you can buy Real Estate, even without having money.

There are many reasons:

- First because they are very safe. They cannot be destroyed and they cannot be stolen so easily. However, 95% of people who do poorly with Real Estate are because they chose a bad tenant. For that reason they cut their payments and they cannot finish paying their own expenses. If you choose your tenant well, I can promise you that in your life, you have met many people who pay well and on time, and very few who pay poorly. In other words, most people pay, because no one wants to be sued, or for a judge to call them for a trial and for his children to see that they are being kicked out of their home through a judicial process. People seek to be calm, give our children the greatest security and not have problems with the law. So Real Estate is almost always safe if you know how to handle it and find good tenants.

- They are valued. In the high or low market, if you buy well, Real Estate is always going to be worth more. They may have peaks, economies have peaks, but ultimately, you can sit back and over time your Real Estate will appreciate. Is it the same with the business you have now? Maybe not, because if you don't work it every day, it's likely to sink. And even if you work hard every day, a new technology may throw you off the market.

- Its valuation does not pay taxes. Actually, you do pay the valuation tax, but it is minimal. On the other hand, if you have a Society or a company, and you have a profit of X, the Treasury will ask you for the proportional part of that profit. It may happen that your utility is in inventory, in creditors or in receivables, so it is not about money that you really have in your pocket, but the treasury is not interested in that and requires its tax share by law.

- They are a good guarantee to find financing. Imagine an 80-year-old woman who takes out a loan at the bank, indicating that she owns an apartment building, she is exempt from paying a mortgage, and receives a monthly income of $ 20,000. Instead, imagine now another younger person, willing, eager to succeed and owner of her own business with a turnover of $ 500,000 per year. Who do you think will get the loan first? Exactly, the old lady. Why? Because Real Estate is an excellent guarantee to grow financially. In fact, there are strategies to use creditworthiness wisely to get into debt. At this point Robert Kiyosaki talks about good credit and bad credit.

- Once you learn to manage them, they are very easy to handle.

- They cannot be wasted

- You can start producing passive income even if they have not finished paying. Personally, I have acquired properties in which the first month, I have not yet paid the mortgage to the bank, and I am already receiving a check with a positive income. Is not it wonderful? Receive a message every month where you see that the tenant has religiously paid his monthly payment. Now, this does not mean that it is easy or overnight, but it requires a plan and strategies that we will see later.

It may be that you currently own your own business, however, when things are going well in a business, we have to inject more money because it is growing, and when it is going bad, we also have to put money in because things are going bad for us. On the other hand, if we manage the Real Estate properly, it is only necessary to make a simple calculation to keep it growing and contribute a moderate amount of income, so that your wealth is organized in a very healthy way.

Chapter 3 - You don't need to be rich to build wealth with Real Estate

You do not need to have a large estate to grow with Real Estate. In fact, people who wait to have money to grow with Real Estate, never manage to do it, since they never get to have money.

Therefore, an estate is created with determination.

The first thing you should know, and it is something in relation to personal development, is that you must assume your responsibility, in this way you will be the owner of your personal power.

We said we were going to talk investor thinking. In this sense, if you tell yourself that your economic situation is bad, either because your partner stole you, or because you were born into a very poor family, or because the market is not favoring you, we all sometimes have moments when Those of us whose life hits us very hard, but if year after year I have the same script of the complaint, perhaps it is something that should change first.

So, to change your financial situation, the first thing you should do is reflect with yourself and think: I am where I am because of my responsibility.

In other words, the good you have achieved is because of your responsibility, as well as the bad. It is true that the market, the global economic context or the partner could affect in a certain way, but the final result is your responsibility.

If you assume your own responsibility, you will have the ability to respond to any difficult situation and emerge victorious thanks to your personal power.

When you answer, it means that you have the ability to give a solution to something specific. It is something tremendously liberating when you are able to take responsibility for something and give it a solution, without looking for blame or excuses.

No matter how many mistakes you've made, always respond with your own personal power.

The other fundamental key to changing your current financial situation is determination. That is, you must be clear that you want and want to get out of where you are now. Many people just talk about what they want, but they never do anything to change their lives. And do you know why? Because they are somehow making a positive profit from the situation they are in. Perhaps it is their safety zone, where they know that at the end of the month they receive a fixed salary of $ 800, even if it is a toxic situation. What these people do not know is that by crossing that poisonous comfort zone, they can find much more lucrative earnings. Of course, they must break with that false sense of security that prevents them from moving in the direction they want.

When we have faith and determination to do something, we don't make cheap excuses that put brakes on our feet. Rather, determination breaks any excuse and clears the way, frees us from any limiting beliefs, and empowers us.

If you are one of those who had the determination to do anything to provide the best future for your children, did you make up an excuse to get ahead? Did you think that the moment was not the ideal one to act? I think not. In fact, I could swear that you thought just the opposite, even though the situation, your economy or the context in general was not aligned in your same direction.

I don't think you doubted that you were going to make it. I don't think you would think something like: "I'm going to try to raise my children." Rather, the thought of someone with determination is of the type: "I am going to raise my children, no matter what."

Determination is a state of security in which it does not matter what happens to you, it does not matter the context, what others say or what happens in your life. You do what you have to do without hesitation. That is the strength of being able to assume your own personal power.

Finally, it is necessary to have Financial Education. It is not enough to have determination and responsibility for your results, you need to educate yourself on a financial level. Without this it is like having a cart tied by horses at full speed, but with blindfolds. In the end it will crash into the first wall.

For this reason, many people who decide to start their own businesses, adopt a determined position where they decide to abandon their salaries, sell everything and bet on a single idea, something quite naive, because if we do not know the planning or do not have a strategy, we will end up bankrupt or losing much more than I invested.

Determination without financial education is suicide.

Finally, of course action is required. There is no use thinking or wanting to do something, if in the end we do not put it into practice.

It is always better to make small changes every day to put ourselves into action, than to completely change our habits and the way we do things in a single day. The power of constancy is much stronger than radical and abrupt change.

When we complain, we lose energy, time, personal power, and self-esteem.

An investor never wants to be with people who are complaining all the time.

The complaint is something that is only in our thoughts, it is not real.

The first thing you need is:

1. Create Income

There are thousands of ways to create them. You will also need to create a spending budget. No one can grow financially if you end up spending more than you earn. If you want to have an instant increase of 30% per year, can you imagine what you can do right now and that only depends on you? Save that 30%. To do this, make your spending budget and you will realize that 30% of the things you spend your money on are totally expendable. In fact, they are things that you could borrow, or lease, or second-hand, or simply not get them, and that is how you can easily save 30%.

You can also think about saving that $ 2 a day coffee. In the end, being frugal is an incredible way to live to become financially free. Therefore, make your budget and have control of your money.

2. Save

It's not about saving at the end of the year or minimal savings that can be reversed into the smallest unpredictable expense. If I don't have a plan for my money, someone will have it for me. Commit to saving 15% of all the money you start to deposit. Many people think at this point that they don't have enough money to save that 15%. The real question is: if right now your salary were reduced by that same percentage, would you stop paying your expenses? I am afraid the answer is no. Our crazy mind is going to manage to get the money and keep us at our same level of expenses.

Therefore, every time you receive an income, set aside that 15% and to pay yourself first. You will feel an incredible sense of freedom and power because you are in control, contrary to what you can feel being a slave to a salary for which you do not stop working and never end up saving, something that among other things, is very frustrating.

3. Investing in Real Estate

Most people do not conceive that they can get one property per year, however, they cannot simply because they believe it is not possible, or because they have not conceived that thought before.

But what if now you start thinking in this direction?

Remember that in what you focus, it expands, and you begin to think that this reality is possible for you, it is very likely that you end up manifesting the things you want. Now, not only does the human being live from desire, you need the other ingredients that we have seen before, but it all begins with the idea that what you think is possible. So I suggest that you start thinking like an investor who sees opportunities as very real, not as something far away and within the reach of only a few. Start analyzing properties, asking about prices, comparing, visiting places where they are being offered, talking to people within the sector, taking photos of the properties, feeling that everything is real, and that you too can buy such a property, if you want it first.

If you propose to buy a property per year, do you think you could achieve it? I bet so. And if it is not a year, it will be in two. And later, with the income from the property, you save it again to reinvest it in Real Estate. One of the biggest of the people who own properties is that they tend to spend the rents, so they do not have cash to pay for the maintenance of the property.

This does not lead to anything other than a bad property and tenants against you, so the Real Estate business will always go badly for you.

As an extreme to this situation, you probably have to mortgage the house due to your mismanagement and the lack of payments from your tenants, with which you end up selling your property for nothing.

Therefore, to make a good savings and spending budget, identify all the income you receive, and instead of thinking about what you can spend it on, think about how you can reduce your expenses to the maximum and how you can invest that money in Real Estate. The idea is that you can reinvest the income of your Real Estate in the purchase of more Real Estate.

There are people who think that receiving an income of $ 80 a month for a small abandoned house is nothing. But if you stop and think about it, you can see that that income turns into $ 960 a year. Think that the same amount of money can be equivalent to 15 more days of vacation.

Do you like this last idea better? The same happens with the 80 dollars of the house, only that we tend to underestimate the power of this type of income because we are not able to extrapolate the results to longer periods of time, so we limit ourselves to the results of the here and now and we devalue what we have.

4. Reinvest

Therefore it is important that the income that we obtain from the Real Estate that we have obtained can be reinvested in the purchase of more Real Estate.

5. Passive Income

In the end we will build a Real Estate equity that has paid for itself, and that over time only leaves us a positive net income in our pocket.

Remember that financial freedom is not achieved with what you win, the game is won by increasing equity and passive income as much as you can.

I do not know anyone who with a single salary has been able to get rich. In fact, I do know rich people who achieved their Financial Freedom by buying Real Estate.

Poor thinking is always talking about what you have earned in the last year based on your salary. However, the thinking of rich is not talking about what you earned with your salary, but about what you were able to grow your wealth in the last year.

If you have a high salary but every time you receive money you end up spending it, you have to learn to manage your wealth in order to retain it as part of your wealth, otherwise you will not be thinking like rich people do, but acting like people poor.

So focus on how much your wealth grew, not how much you've earned. Think if in 10 years you can talk about your salary now as something important in the future, unless you do something with that salary now to increase your wealth in 10 years.

No matter what salary you start with, in the end it is about always applying the way of thinking of rich people: save a part of your income, invest it in property and reinvest the profits to grow your wealth.

When you start saving, you can feel like you are in control, and you can feel like you are in control of your spending. This is when you start to make different financial decisions. You start meeting with different people and when you least expect it you are doing business that you could not imagine at this moment. It is not a magic formula, but a simple but powerful way of thinking, to grow your wealth like rich people do.

Let me tell you a curious story. It is about a butler of one of the richest people in Argentina. The owner of the mansion paid an almost paltry salary to the butler for all the work he did. However, the servant always tried to set aside a little salary and save it. In fact, every time his friends went out for beers, he took care of his money and invested it in buying small assets, like pigs. When he managed to buy several of these pigs, he was able to sell them for a money that allowed him to acquire the first property of him. It was not a large farm, but a small piece of land of only about 300 square meters.

However, he was able to rent that small piece of land as a vegetable garden to the owner of a neighboring farmhouse, with which he was able to reinvest the rental proceeds to buy an even larger piece of land.

This is how now, the butler who received a small salary in that mansion, is now one of the richest people in Argentina.

He has been able to purchase top-notch apartment blocks and land, and live fully off his income. However, he started out poor, or at least income level. What many people ignore is that despite him receiving a small salary, in his mind thoughts of a rich person were created. This is how he was able to get out of his poverty situation and become rich.

But it is not the only case, there are thousands of people who could acquire their first properties in Real Estate starting from a simple salary.

The proof that this is possible indicates that it does not matter how much money you are now making with your salary, but the way of thinking you have installed in your mind and how you manage your own money.

The paradigm that I want to give you with this chapter is that the price of a property depends on the owner's need.

The price of a property is not objective. If a family has just bought a property where the children are happy, the couple is happy and everything is fine, while another house, of the same size and quality right next to the first, belongs to a family with marital problems on the verge of get divorced, which house is cheaper? The second, even if it is of better quality than the first. Therefore, consumer thinking sees only the price, while investor thinking sees the owner's need and motivation.

For what reason does the owner want to get rid of his property?

The person may want to sell at a fixed price and do not look for another negotiation option, so it is possible that doing business with this person is complicated, since he is not influenced by any other motivation that could make him lower the price.

Always try to find the worst house in the best neighborhood, because that is the great opportunity to be able to revalue the house and make something with little value, become a great asset.

Now, why do people sell at a discount? I mean, why would someone want to sell his property at a lower price than the market dictates?

There are several reasons:

- Because the person urgently needs the money

- For a divorce

- Due to illness

- For a transfer

- For an inheritance that the owner wishes to get rid of

- Bad administration

There are many reasons that can cause someone to sell his property badly. It is important to be financially prepared to be able to withstand any blow that life gives us, in economic terms, and that allows us to be able to keep our properties, or at most sell them at the price that the market really dictates.

Now, this does not mean that you take advantage of anyone. There is no long-term business that takes advantage of people's plight. It is rather the opposite, that is to help people sell their properties in a way that we all win.

In fact, our credibility is worth much more than our money. Businesses are not created by taking advantage of people, but are created and maintained by creating a solution that favors both parties.

Look for properties in poor condition, or undervalued, in upscale areas. In this way, what for a consumer is just a property in poor condition, for an investor it is a great opportunity to do good business.

This is how most Real Estate investors have made their fortunes. They have been able to see beyond the simple image of a property in poor condition, to see the opportunity behind that first impression. Having the ability to imagine how you can value something is what makes wealthy people grow.

Do not look for luxuries at a low price because it will not be the normal thing you can find. Start by looking for properties that apparently nobody wants, but that you know that you can increase their value. Get trained in revaluation techniques, attend events about buying and selling homes and learn how to use financing from the homeowner himself.

Not only can the bank grant you a mortgage, anyone with money can. Make an attempt and talk to the tenant of the property if he would be willing to finance the payment, so that you can pay it in monthly installments and not in cash.

Now, in what other ways can you finance yourself without the intermediation of a bank?

If you are one of those who thinks that nobody is going to give you a penny, then you have consumer thinking. It is time to change your mindset for that of an investor. I mean that it is possible to get financing in different ways if you know how, and without the intermediation of a bank.

You can finance yourself thanks to the property owner, and establish a period to pay off the debt. I personally know someone who secured financing from the property owner for 15 years, with interest half lower than what the banks were then offering.

Another of the most recent cases that I have met is another person who has obtained two central properties in Barcelona, each with 12 rooms, and with financing from the owner.

Therefore, it is possible to get homes at a very low cost, with discounts of 30% or more, if you manage to discover which homes are for sale and that need to be revalued, but that it is in a good area. In addition, the owner can take over the loan of your home if you manage to agree with him a financing plan for X years, always with an interest percentage much lower than that of the banks. You will be surprised to realize the number of people who are willing to get rid of their properties as soon as possible, at very low prices and who are even willing to charge a monthly fee as payment, while the rest of the amount allows you to finance it at your own cost.

That is, this type of purchase is similar to if someone only asked you for a monthly rent for their property, with the right to purchase, with the great difference in your favor that from the first moment you are the owner of the property, and you can rent it or do what you want, even resell it. In this way what you get is simply to pay the value of the property while you use it, at the same time that you can make use of it and exploit it economically.

Trust me, you don't need to be a skilled trader to do this. You can get properties to do this yourself, if you focus on doing it and commit to it.

Chapter 6 - The Real Estate Business Is Done By Buying, Not By Selling

Most poor-thinking people think:

"I will try to sell my property for a value greater than the purchase price, and thus I will earn an extra."

But it is not about earning an extra. In fact, that extra may simply be the margin in the market devaluation. That is, it may be that when you sell a home they give you an amount higher than the price you paid for it, but if you want to buy a similar home you may be surprised to see that the purchase price is precisely the same value, so You did not earn anything, you simply turned your home into a liquid asset, in cash, but you did not make a profitable business.

What really matters is the time of home purchase in which you should think about saving that 30% or even 50% of its original value.

Therefore, profits are always made at the time of purchase, not on sale. When you think this way and are able to get homes with deep discounts at the time of purchase, you free yourself from what the market can do because you have already done a great deal by buying at a good price.

The price of homes would have to vary a lot for a purchase at 50% of its original value to cease to be profitable.

The same happens with tenants, the business is in the good acquisition of people who pay their rents religiously and are responsible with their monthly payments, at that moment you are ensuring that you will have stable income.

The real question is: why do many people lose their properties?

The answer is simple: because they don't study their numbers in detail.

There will always be someone who will tell you that they know someone who did badly in Real Estate, and that they lost everything. Perhaps that person did not do his calculations well and allowed himself to be sold for the first construction project that was presented to him with great appeal.

However, negotiating correctly in Real Estate is not simply about saving money to buy the first project that a seller tries to sneak up on you. You need to do the profitability calculations to see if that property can really be a profitable business or not.

It is not surprising that many people who embark on Real Estate without a detailed analysis find that after making the acquisition, they are not receiving the income they were promised, and this can happen for several reasons:

- Because no one was clear about the property management costs

- Because they did not inform him of the charges or debts that this Root Good may carry.

Now this is not the fault of the agent who sold you the property, but of yourself. It is your responsibility as the owner of your own business to study the numbers correctly and to be able to discern the wheat from the chaff.

Study the numbers of the property you want to acquire and see if it really is a profitable business. Take into account all the expenses that you may incur and ask for all the official documentation detailing such current expenses.

Therefore, an investor, rather than looking at the property, what he looks at are the numbers themselves. What does it matter if the property is beautiful or not? Or if it's just a bathroom in New York? Or a mansion on Everest? Perhaps the best option is a bathroom in New York even if you personally don't like living there.

Think that you do not have to make use of those properties. You don't even have to like it. They simply must be profitable businesses in which the numbers are in your favor.

You never know if that property will be your personal home, what really matters is that it leaves you an income. That in itself is the Real Estate business.

Always looking for properties to pay for themselves. It is the same with children, a father or mother is successful when they get their children to stay alone, otherwise we have not created an independent being.

With the properties we look for exactly the same thing, that the income from the rent itself pays the mortgage, insurance, maintenance, taxes and any other expenses. So that the net balance of the property is always positive and in our favor.

There are those who think that a property that can pay for itself does not exist in their country or is difficult to find, and the reason is always the same: they have not searched enough.

Surely, if you live near a big city or in the center of it, you will be surrounded by thousands of houses. It is very likely that after a year there will be offers of homes that could be a great deal. All you need is to seek them out with determination.

Up to this point, are you sure that it is now possible to acquire real estate and do great business?

I remember that day when I was traveling with my wife to the center of Madrid. Just as the taxi to the destination was picking us up, I asked him if he knew of anyone in the area who sold any property. To my surprise, the driver nodded and told me about different apartments that were for sale.

At that moment I asked him about the price of those houses, and that was when he decided to call the owner of the same directly to spend with him.

When we started our conversation, the first thing I did was ask him how long his apartments had been for sale. Remember that what determines the value of a real estate is always the need to sell it by the owner.

He told me that they had been in the market for a long time and that the reason for getting rid of them was that he did not receive income from sales as before. In other words: he could not rent them, a fact that he liked, since he indicated to me the fundamental need that this person had to sell those properties as soon as possible.

I then asked him if with a down payment for the house, he would be willing to finance the rest of the balance, to which he replied that it would be possible.

Now imagine how much time I spent making that loan, compared to what I could spend if I asked for the same money at a bank, with the added interest that financial institutions require from their clients.

In addition to all the documentation and information that a bank requires from its clients, it is likely that in the end they will not end up granting you the loan.

Instead, the owner of this property was a retired man who urgently needed money, wanted to get rid of a property in poor condition, and wanted at all costs to have a monthly income that would help him pay his own expenses, so the option Buying his home under his own financing was not bad for him, in fact it was quite the opposite, something highly attractive for his situation at that time.

Now, why do you think that these types of opportunities are not usually found so easy by people? Simply because they are not looking hard enough. If you only contact 3 people, it is likely that you will not find the opportunity you were looking for. On the other hand, if you contact 600 people, I can assure you that you will begin to see opportunities where you previously thought impossible.

Therefore, always look for the same owner to finance the debt. Make a lease with an option to buy that allows you to have the property from the first moment by just paying an amount similar to a monthly rent.

But you do not have to be the owner of the home to do business in Real Estate, you can also act as an intermediary in purchase-sale transactions. To do this, identify what land or homes are for sale in your neighborhood or town, and make contacts with people who are willing to invest in those properties.

When you have identified both parties, connect them to close the deal. You will get a good commission for closing the deal without having invested a dollar in the process. It is a zero cost business, in which only your ability to connect with people, present different properties and facilitate the buying and selling process intervenes.

Now this takes time. It's not as easy as going outside one afternoon and closing a deal the next day. You need to be patient, research the market, and make mistakes to find out what works and what doesn't. You may be able to close a big deal after a year, but just doing one of these transactions can earn you a big commission for the rest of your life, if the property's value is high enough to give you a high commission. This process can sometimes seem slow, but believe me it will pay off if you are a determined person and have the security of wanting to change your finances.

I invite you to take into account the following:

- Value what you have

- Trust yourself

- Take the time to educate yourself financially

- Act despite fear

- Learn continuously

It is very important that you are a trustworthy person who values the power of the word. When you start doing business in Real Estate and the people around you see that you are someone of your word, they will have no problem investing with you and trusting you. At this moment perhaps not, because now you have no experience, but as soon as you start to get into this business, each time acquiring new properties becomes a simpler process.

Acquiring the first property is always more difficult. The second somewhat easier. The third even more. And so on. If you follow this process and do not give up on the way, you will be surprised how easy it can be to do business in Real Estate, and the amount of properties that you can acquire and that now you do not even imagine possible.

Most surprising of all, anyone can walk this path, as long as you take responsibility for what happens in your life and are determined to run this business.

The second important point on the list is to believe in yourself, even if you don't. This means that sometimes you will have to deal with your mental chatter that is always trying to make you feel small, or insecure, or ashamed. Phrases like:

- But where do you think you're going?

- Who would want to do business with you?

- Who will trust you?

- Do you really think you are up to the task of this business?

- Have you not thought about retiring and dedicating yourself to other things?

- You are going to waste all your money

- You don't have enough experience

- You are not good enough at this

- You are going to ruin

- Keep your money and don't take risks

- You don't believe in yourself

- You don't speak well

Do these phrases sound familiar to you? So it happens to you like 95% of the people who start doing business in Real Estate. Keep in mind that all these phrases are just thoughts, but they are not reality. Do you think you really are not worth enough? Or that you are not prepared to do this business? Of course not. It's just your mind trying to trip you to stay in your comfort zone, where everything is safe. However, once you get rid of fear, you will begin to tame your subconscious. Fear is an emotion that paralyzes people and makes them feel without resources. Every human being could develop incredible potential in any area if he took the time to eliminate his limiting beliefs of what is or is not possible.

In the end they are just unreal ideas or subjective interpretations of reality, but it is not reality itself. They are just your thoughts. I encourage you to question them, question them, and take action to show your subconscious what reality is.

The third point is to educate yourself financially. In fact, I encourage you to pay to do so. There are people who cost much more money, including health or a marriage, not having financial education, not because they do not want to be good parents, or good husbands or wives, or good businessmen, or not because they do not have ambition or want to prosper financially, they just didn't have the mental skills or the simple rules of the financial business, to face such a challenge and they lost everything.

So remember this concept: the difference is always made by financial education. If you are reading this book right now, I can already sense two things about you:

1. There is a part of you that wants to grow financially

2. There is another part that says that you can, otherwise you would not be reading this page, nor would you have had the determination to acquire this copy.

How many businesses that passed through your hands could you have taken advantage of if you had had this education?

Perhaps you can realize now the amount of business and opportunities that you have missed just because of that.

How much would you have earned in your life if you had known this information before?

Can you see how what you now know has opened your eyes?

How much would you have helped your relatives or close friends save or earn if you had known this information?

Perhaps your children want to live in the house of their dreams and make a large investment to get it. However, I suggest that you first make them think if that property is a good investment, and if it would not be a better idea to rent it. They can even rent a mansion for a weekend to have the experience and to realize that to go to the bathroom it is not necessary to travel almost half a kilometer.

Many times we get carried away by what we desire in our hearts but with little logical judgment. It is important to think about whether or not what we are about to acquire may be a good economic investment in the future. On the contrary, think about how to find a property that a priori is not the house of your dreams, but that you can acquire at low cost and transform it into whatever you want. That would be an investor thought and not a consumer one.

Personally, I have had the experience of living in large houses and I know that in the end I end up using a small part of the house. I usually leave everything scattered in all corners and then it becomes very difficult for me to find the objects throughout the house. In my opinion, you don't need a mansion to live happily or in the house of your dreams.

If you want to live the experience of living in the house of your dreams for a while, rent the property and after a while decide if you would really be willing to acquire it.

For this reason, it is important to think about what you really need and how to find the best investment, always trying to do business with people who are motivated to get rid of their properties as soon as possible and who are in good neighborhoods.

Take the time to contact people or people who can inform you about properties for sale. Talk to the owners of those properties and ask them questions to find out what their motivation is for wanting to sell, in this way you can get great discounts that you would not think possible, even financing by the owner of the house himself, so that you only have to pay one monthly rent by way of rent, with a much lower commission than what a bank could offer you, and with the addition that from the first moment you can make use of the property, even rent it and start earning income.

Now, it is important that you do your numbers, that you make a detailed calculation of all the expenses that you are going to incur with the acquisition of that property, and if it is worth buying it to put it up for rent. In the end you need to know if the rental income will be higher than the sum of purchase expenses, taxes, insurance, administration expenses and any other added expenses that you should consider.

Make sure that the property does not carry charges of any kind or debts that the previous owner has not paid. Find out if there is no legislation that is about to come into force and that affects in any way the construction of the property.

Chapter 9 - How to grow with Real Estate?

The first thing is to have the determination to do it, followed by a good financial education, along with taking action.

Have you already decided to acquire your first property by reading this information?

Remember that the times you have changed your life have been when you have believed in yourself.

Can you remember a time when you decided not to continue with more of the same in some aspect of your life, and completely change your reality?

That is the power of determination, and it is exactly what you need now to get started in this Real Estate business. It is time to completely change your finances and your level of wealth. It is time to change the way you handle your money and plan for the future so that it depends on you and not on luck.

Keep in mind that these ideas are not reality, they are just thoughts:

- No one will believe in me

- I have no money

- I do not have experience

When you have wanted to do something, you have done it even without money. In other words, not having money is almost always a justification, never a reason. Because when you want to do something, you look for a way to do it whatever it is.

Another of the most common excuses is:

-        I have no time

As with money, when you are determined to do something, you find the time to do it. Almost magically you start to have unlimited resources to do what you want. So, find the money and time you need now to do what you want.

Another reason we give ourselves for not taking action is:

- The information is free on the internet

And although it is true, there is a lot of free information on the internet, there is also a lot of garbage and people who try to induce financial panic and fill us with fear. They always try to make us believe that the world is going to end, that everything is about to go bankrupt and that a great economic crisis is coming. All this only increases that feeling of lack of resources, that mental chatter in your mind that makes you feel insecure, and in the end you end up paralyzed, without taking action and without taking responsibility for your finances and your own life.

Would you like to end up financially disempowered? I bet not. In fact, many families are brought up with a tragic mentality, in which everything looks like it will get worse tomorrow. If that is your case, I invite you to reflect if all this is true. Do you hear these types of comments in your family or on television?

- Something very serious is going to happen in this country

- A great economic disaster is coming

- This is not the time to do business now

- It is financial suicide to buy right now

In fact, almost always the countries are getting better, the schools are getting better, the hospitals, the roads.

It is time to leave catastrophic thinking behind and start to believe more in yourself, despite what others try to make you believe of what reality is, and what is or is not possible for you. It is only up to you to do what you want.

On the other hand, look for a mentor who is already where you want to go. Take the time to meet people who are in the Real Estate business, ask them how much they earn, how they carry out their operations, you can even assess whether working for a time as an employee in this type of business would be a good idea to know in depth how the real estate works and gain grassroots experience. In this way, you can contemplate approaching real estate agencies of farms, land or houses to leave your curriculum, and work for them for a few months with the aim of learning everything you can, observe how this sector works from within, have contacts that otherwise Perhaps you could not get to know and have an idea of how property prices move, discounts, how negotiations work, reform budgets, the laws applicable to the sale of homes and their management, as well as profitability analysis of this type of project.

However, none of this is strictly necessary to start the Real Estate business right away, you can start from today to search for properties through sales portals, to contact the owners and communicate with them.

You can even take a walk through the neighborhoods of the cities that you like the most and that have growth potential. See what properties are for sale and write down their phone numbers. Call the owners and have a fluid conversation, without pressure, you can even pretend to be the friend or cousin of the really interested one, in this way you can stay on the sidelines of the business and remain calm during the conversation, at the same time that you can draw Very valuable information about everything that the owner will have to tell you. It is your time to find out if it is possible to finance yourself by the property owner, at what terms and with what interest, what type of discount they would be willing to take. Find out the price level in the area to estimate a monthly rental income. Enter platforms for the sale or rental of homes and do a search as a potential client to find out the prices that are handled in the area. Investigate the evolution of housing and rent prices in the area. Visit real estate agencies that can give you more information, posing as someone interested in buying or renting one. Make contacts with these people and begin to open the range of possibilities and contacts.

Another of the typical excuses that people often say to themselves when they are about to start a Real Estate business is:

-       It is very expensive…

The real question is: which is more expensive, education or ignorance?

It is too expensive not to educate yourself. It's a bit like thinking about going to the hospital when your broken arm has gotten better. What good is it then? The time to educate yourself financially is now, right now, not when you have money. Or thoughts of the type:

- I will buy this home when I get out of this crisis

- I will buy this farm when I have more money

However, the time will never come to have more money, if you do not act now to get it with the information in this reading.

In fact, it is in times of crisis when we need more education to get out of it. We cannot solve a problem with the same mindset that created it. So, it is time to transform and consider alternatives that make us progress financially from education.

Getting educated is the starting point for the transformation of your finances. Choose a good mentor who can give you the information and education you need. I encourage you to continue training after finishing this reading, and not to give up in the process. The rewards can be incredible if you are determined not to give up. It is true, you can find many mediocre training courses, even bad ones on financial education, but there are also many others that are excellent, and that will be the turning point in your finances.

Remember this phrase:

"A madman without results is a madman, a madman with results is a genius"

The difference between both crazy is what you speak to the world. Talking is easy. Business is easy and can even be done on a napkin. The differential point is the commitment you have with yourself to carry them out. Are you committed to making those small changes that from now on will change your life?

In my personal life I have had the bad luck to see how one of my close relatives suffered from alcohol addiction. And I can assure you that an addiction not only changes the life of the person who suffers from it, but also that of 10 people around him.

In the same way, if you change your life and become a prosperous person, not only you change, you will be changing the lives of 10 other people around you. Always think about giving your children an investor education, not a consumer. What do you want to do? However, in order to educate them as investors, you first need to think like one. It's about changing your life. Look at the number of people you can change if you decide to change your personal finances.

Keep this phrase in mind:

"Chasing the game without a guide leads to the undergrowth"

If from today you want to grow financially, but decide to do it alone, it is likely that you will have to face situations that are complex to solve. I suggest you seek help from a mentor who is where you want to go.

That is why it is important that you choose the right person to train you financially.

Chapter 10 - Final Conclusions

1. Is it better to buy financed or cash?

It will always be better to buy financed if the numbers of the profitability calculation always come out in your favor. Always keep in mind that the capital deposit you make each month, plus the financial cost of that monthly loan, is less than the rental income, discounting any other administration and property management expenses.

2. Why is it better to finance yourself than to pay in cash?

Imagine that you have $ 100,000 and you want to buy a nice property. It is a better idea to buy four and start paying them monthly, than to buy one and pay it in cash to pay off your debt. In the end, over time you will have four properties in your name, while the other way you will have only one although you will start receiving net income from minute one.

Also, if you get those four properties to pay for themselves each month, you can have infinite leverage. In other words, each property will pay for itself independently, without having to inject any of your own capital.

3. Is it a good idea to partner with someone you trust to invest in Real Estate?

It is important to create a team to do business in Real Estate, because it is just almost impossible. You will always need a bank or some lenders or investors. You will also need partners or people who can invest with you. One of the problems of people who have a lot of liquidity is that this liquid cash is not paying them enough interest and they want to invest them in businesses that give them a good return. Now, anyone is not going to let you manage their money, you must first earn the trust of people and for this you must show that you know how to do business. And this is only achieved if you first do your own business using your capital.

4. Is it preferable to buy in the project phase or when it is already built?

Personally, I don't like to buy in the construction phase. If I had to choose between giving an entry now for a house that will begin to be profitable two years in the future, when the house is ready, or buying a property at this time that is already ready to be rented and start receiving income, I prefer without hesitation the second option.

What is the use of leveraging your money without giving you a return for two years, when you can take advantage of it from today?

In addition, it is not the first case of a builder who for some reason abandons the work, and 400 people who invested in those homes are left hanging. The reasons why the project finally cannot go ahead can be several:

- The builder did not have the proper building licenses

-The builder had family problems, divorces or any other situation in which he stopped allying with partners or lost part of his capital

- Or what is worse: the builder disappeared with all the money and everything was a scam.

In addition, participating in this type of project means competing with all the investors who bought just when I did, to be able to sell or lease. And that can get complicated, so I have to wait other years to let the property price go up, so I can get rid of it.

5. If I have little experience in Real Estate, how can I discern what is a good deal and what is not?

The secret is simple, make decisions, rehearse and make mistakes, educate yourself financially. Taking action and making mistakes is the only formula to gain experience in this type of business. It is something similar to what happens when you ride a bicycle. No matter how much theory you try to read in a book about riding a bike, you won't be able to test yourself until you actually do it.

Therefore, knowing the rules, knowing the market, and above all, knowing your own strengths and weaknesses, you must act with all of this and make decisions. It is not a magical process, but it requires determination, taking action and learning from mistakes, while continuing to educate yourself financially.

6. If I currently live in an apartment for which I pay a mortgage and which is an expense for me, how do I go about buying a property with which to obtain a positive income?

These kinds of questions can be asked by many people, and they end up immobilized. If you are a father or mother of a family with several children in your care, perhaps you have not questioned the way in which you were going to manage your work together with the upbringing of your children, or in what way you were going to find the necessary time. You just did it and took out the resources to do it. The same thing happens with this type of situation. Despite having a monthly expense for the mortgage on the house where you currently live, it is important that this situation does not limit you and that you have the determination to start doing business in Real Estate.

Make a spending budget to see what you are spending on right now and what you could save. Do not wait to have all the money available, start saving now but look for properties for sale. You will be amazed to see the amount of opportunities that could be within your reach with just the savings you can have. What if one morning you woke up and decided to go to work when all the traffic lights were green? You will most likely never make it to work. The normal thing is that you go out despite the fact that you will have to stop at several traffic lights, and when you do you will have to make decisions to know which direction to follow. That is why it is important to get out as soon as possible and make your own plan.

Remember this: no matter your personal situation, you can make a difference and change your life if you are determined to do so. It all depends on your mind.

7. Is it a good idea to buy land on the outskirts of a city and try to sell it in the future even if it is not buildable?

This could be a more complex issue than it seems, since this type of investment depends a lot on the type of personality and the investment strategy of the person who decides to carry it out.

In addition, buying land requires a lot of liquidity because if you cannot use it as a crop or for another purpose that generates income, that land will only cost you. And your priority from the first moment is to always generate a positive cash flow, liquidity or passive income. This does not mean that you do not embark on this type of project, but I would advise you to start looking for business opportunities that always from the first moment generate a passive income that covers all expenses.

Thank you very much for making it to the end. I invite you to continue training financially.

And remember: if you have not bought a property today, it has been because you simply did not want to.

Have a wonderful day!

* 9 7 9 8 5 4 7 5 0 1 1 4 2 *